ROSE TILLEMANS,

# I'm Still Dai

D0439743

## Praying through Good Days and Bad

# TWENTY-THIRD PUBLICATIONS

185 WILLOW STREET • PO BOX 180 • MYSTIC, CT 06355
TEL: 1-800-321-0411 • FAX: 1-800-572-0788
E-MAIL: ttpubs@aol.com • www.twentythirdpublications.com

Bayard

**Second printing 2003**

Cover illustration: "Red Dress Dancing," by Anna
Copyright ©2000; All rights reserved. www.annaoneglia.com

Twenty-Third Publications
A Division of Bayard
185 Willow Street
P.O. Box 180
Mystic, CT 06355
(860) 536-2611
(800) 321-0411
www.twentythirdpublications.com

ISBN:1-58595-237-0
Library of Congress Catalog Card Number: 2002109052
Printed in the U.S.A.

# Contents

# Foreword

I never met Rose Tillemans face to face. We met instead by mail. She sent me ten of her prayers wondering if they might be published. I thought they had promise and encouraged her to write forty or so, enough to fill a little book. My first thought was that Rose's prayers would be perfect for older women who are dealing with the same issues that challenged Rose: fatigue, a body that won't cooperate, loneliness, and sometimes discouragement. I thought that older women religious in particular might take comfort and inspiration from Rose's prayers.

Though I still think this is true, I have since learned that Rose was more than an elderly nun. (See the brief autobiography at the end of this book). She was an activist with deep convictions about peace and justice. She had a great affinity for the poor and homeless and eventually founded Peace House where the poor could gather and be welcome.

And she suffered from depression, a circumstance that makes all that she accomplished extraordinary. In these prayers, her depression is an underlying theme. She struggled to keep her dark feelings from oppressing others, especially the Peace House community. And so, Rose's prayers will be a comfort as well to those who suffer with depression.

What comes through, in spite of the foibles of old age and the difficulties of depression is a free spirit yearning to be with God. Rose was young at heart, very much in love with God, and she took great joy in all that God created—from a tiny African violet to the great blue sky above her.

And, of course, Rose loved to dance. She died on July 5, 2002, but I would like to think that Rose is still dancing, a beloved partner of the God of the dance.

—Gwen Costello, Publisher

# I'm Still Dancing

## Praying Through
## Good Days and Bad

# Introduction

I'm hitting eighty, and I look it. This does not bother me because old age has lots of perks. The wrinkles grooved into my face proclaim honesty. I still have quite a lively step and can get to work and to many parts of town on the city bus for fifty cents. Lively music prompts me to dance, whether mundane or holy.

Several times a week, the Sacred Energizer pushes my start button and moves me to my great love, Peace House. This storefront community in inner-city Minneapolis has welcomed poor and homeless people into its friendly space with dignity and affirmation for seventeen years. These survivors of poverty and politics have been "professors" for me. My prayer continues to be that mutual mentoring between the poor and the economically comfortable will someday bring about structural change.

My passion for living is also sustained by my birth family, hardy and hearty friends, causes and communities, among them my St. Stephen's Church Community, always fresh and feisty. I am a Sister of St. Joseph of Carondelet, an order which has for fifty-five years called me to be sister to the "dear neighbor without distinction."

John Ruskin once wrote, "Religion is everywhere around me. It opens to my imagination spiritual beauty and holiness." I embrace these words as though I had written them myself. The title of this little book captures that spirit as well; it is the spirit with which I try to face life. My desire is to embrace all that is forgiving, hopeful, happy, serendipitous, sacred, wondrous, welcoming, miraculous, and magnificent.

Through all of this I'm still dancing, and I'm hoping that through these prayers, you, my readers, will want to join the dance. No matter what obstacles, setbacks, down days you are facing, God, the great leader of the dance, is with you inviting you to join the sacred dance of life, today and for the rest of your life.

# 1. You Are God
## of the Dance

Good morning, Holy God.
I give thanks for my upbeat
awakening this morning.
When I got in gear I turned on the radio
which was playing "Come home, come home.
Don't write, don't call. I just want you home."
I spun around my space with total abandon,
felt giddy and a bit dizzy when the song ended.
Lightsome music always prompts me to dance.
Some heartbeats are skipped, a raising of the pulse.
Yet, we are told to sing and dance—
"make a joyful sound unto God,"
no matter how old we are.
Call it prayer, I say.
Dear God of the Dance, I'm 79
and I'm grateful to still be dancing.
When I sit in my all-purpose chair
and listen to music on the radio

I also feel called to mindfulness of you, Holy One.
The saints of times past went into levitation.
The difference between them and me
is that they stayed up for a long time,
against all laws of gravity.
I don't have that gift.
If I did, someone would design a shrine around me,
and people would come from all over
just to observe me.
Soon sweet aromas would pour forth.
No thanks.
All I ask of you, Holy Morning God,
is to keep me upbeat this day, dancing in my heart.

# 2. You Are My Energizer

Free-Spirited Energizer, I just came from
a walk this early fall morning,
and I saw you everywhere along my path.
The fading cool moon was a thin slice
of white against a blue sky.
Overnight, a fully clothed maple tree,
my joy for so many weeks,
had been wind-stripped of its golden-red attire.
I was startled at first, but I also appreciated
the beauty in its bare starkness.
I studied the tree's sparse shape and gave thanks
for its barren graceful outline against
a red brick apartment building.
I can't change the tree back to autumn glory,
but I can re-adjust my concept
of where beauty now lies.
God, you were in the wind. You were the wind.
May this early morning calm and delight
sustain me this day, O Free-Spirited Energizer.

# 3. You Are God of My Heart

It's 2:30 a.m. and I cannot sleep, God of My Heart.
No point in trying to force it.
Something in me is blocking it.
It could be rage or the need to control.
I leave my bed and began to swirl
around my living space in dance.
I stop to focus on my print
of the Picasso Peace Dance.
What free spirits and supple
body movements these dancers have.
How lithe their yielding bodies,
their playful let-go movements.
They are holding hands and extending
palm branches to one another.
There is gentle playfulness
as they encircle the peace dove.
Their bodies bend as they spring.
What nonconformists they are!

In my own dance, Comforter God,
I try to imitate the Peace People in the print.
I attempt to be supple and loose-jointed.
As I push my hands against the air,
releasing the stiffness in my neck and shoulders,
I direct it out the window.
Over and over I call out to you, God of my Heart.
When I become limp with exhaustion,
I fall into bed and close my eyes.
But I know I will wake up at six; I always do,
so I will only have three hours of sleep.
I recall a Peace House incident of many years back.
It happened in our meditation circle.
When Connie's time came to speak,
she told of her fierce attack of anxiety and said, "Sometimes
all I can do is wait for it to pass."
Perhaps this solution might work
for me as the day unfolds.
Comforter God,
I ask just to be with you today,
just to stay in your presence.

# 4. You Are My Restorer

Holy One, this evening I hold in my heart
tears of exhaustion and pain. I am without a voice.
My left ear and head ache.
My throat is sore when I speak.
I feel within me anxiety beyond my control.
"It's time for you 'furies' to leave me alone!" I pray.
Suddenly I remember a response
to a litany we recited in my home parish church
so many years ago: "Lord deliver us."
I pray it now to you with fervor
as though I were a child again, leaning against
my mother in our family pew, number 26.
I breathe in your healing powers, Holy One,
and exhale my heavy thoughts.
I hop out of my chair and
dance around my space,
willing away the furies and beckoning
your healing powers to fill me.

Often when I am angry or anxiety-prone,
my normalcy is restored by the next day.
Even at my age, I still have much to learn about
letting go of things that get me fired up.
And yet I do try to live by
Madonna Kolbenschlag's admonition:
"We must be capable of outrage
for the sake of the reign of God."
But I don't want to cling to my outrage
until it makes me sick.
O Blessed Restorer of Health,
be with me as I attempt to breathe in your holy energy.
You are the One who can move me and strengthen me
until I am able to respond
like the little train in my childhood book:
"I think I can, I think I can."
Blessed are you, my God;
with your help I think I really can.

# 5. You Are the God of Quiet Gifts

Holy God of Peace and Rest,
the sign on the Peace House door reads:
"Closed for two weeks of renovation."
For me, this will be a time to recover lost energy.
I am "vacationing" here in my own space
with what I consider necessary props:
the chair that fits my body so well
for all my sit-down business;
papers, letters, folders piled around me;
the framed Picasso Peace Dance
within view on my wall;
the hand-carved blue bird mobile that faces me
until the breeze from the window
turns her sideways;
a Matisse still life postcard;
and a beloved pink orchid tacked to the wall.

My telephone answering machine says
in my tired squawky voice,
"I'm either away from my phone,
can't hear it, or can't find it."
Bless me and surround me, Great God of Rest.
After my prayer, I yearn to be in our complex pool,
just to float for a while this day.
I look out my window to check:
nobody down there, no sounds at all.
I gratefully prepare to go down and plunge in.
What a treat, O God of pleasures beyond all counting,
what gifts I have to savor!
I give thanks to you as I flip over in the water
and lie motionless seeing only blue skies.
I breath in the sweet, warm end-of-summer day
in total oneness with all that is.
Perhaps this feeling would have been called
abandonment once upon a time,
or it might be called Nirvana today.
God of Quiet Gifts, soothe me during these two weeks.
Slow me down, keep me afloat
in your lovely and restful healing waters.

# 6. You Are the God of Stillness

"Be still and know that I am God," says Psalm 113.
In the same context, I also recall
these words from T.S. Eliot:
"Teach us to care and not to care
Teach us to be still
Even among these rocks,
Our peace is in your will."
I believe that your will for me, O God,
is to be attuned to the Sacred.
I ask of you, Attentive One,
for a sense of your presence this evening.
Help me to absorb reverently the moments
you give me and to find richness and strength in them.
Keep me from moving too fast
from one activity to another.
May I work against a sense of urgency—
that I must be in perpetual motion
because my causes are worthy ones.

Give me the gift of pausing to savor
what is happening now
before I plunge into the next activity.
May I see, hear, and touch each moment attentively.
Time and place are so sacred.
With our country at war, much of the world in combat
with hunger and homelessness,
call me to prayer and thoughtful action.
But for now, Great God of Stillness,
help me to be still.

 # 7. You Are the Holy One

God, present in this summer heat
and torrid temperatures,
I really don't believe that controlling the climate
is in your job description.
But you do sustain me with your care
during all the seasons.

I feel undone tonight by the atmospheric heat
of rage between Sasha and Ben,
which overwhelmed me at Peace House today.
Holy Strengthener, be with them tonight
wherever they are. Hold them, comfort them,
quiet their rage this hot, hot night.
And do the same for me, please.
I feel so weak and shaken.
May tomorrow be cooler and calmer.
I ponder my own spurts of rage
and try to replace them with tenderness of heart
toward those who might do me harm.
I pray this line from Psalm 62:
"Show me your ways, O God and teach me your paths."
I have kept this verse in my repertoire for over 50 years,
no matter where I am theologically.
It's a prayer for all seasons
and it transcends all personal convictions.
Show me your way, Holy One,
your way of peace, forgiveness, and compassion.
May I walk the path you have set for me.

# 8. You Are God of Refreshment

Thank you God, Gracious Giver.
This long weekend is a gift of abundance
away from my daily work-life in the city.
I sit alone on a wooden bench facing a lake
rippling with the sun's last sparkles of daytime splendor.
"How great thou art; I scarce can take it in."
In a day or so this richness will be a memory,
but not a buried treasure.
My body and soul will draw strength
from each blessing of these three days:
the love I see in the couple who built this lake place,
their tender concerned expressions
of one another's joys and pains,
and their extended warmth to me, their guest.
I indulged more freely in the plates, bowls, glasses
of appealing food and drink than I do at home.

Although I am not as tuned in on this weekend
to the world's starvation and poverty as I usually am,
I know in my heart that you, dear Gracious Giver,
want me to feast at this time.
"It is truly right and just," as we used to pray at Mass,
for me to turn to play and rest and to revel
with my dear, long-time friends
who have understood my
"sitting down and my rising up" for so many years.
Blessed are you, Great God of Refreshment!

# 9. You Are Holy Presence

This past week, Holy Presence,
my whole being was totally preoccupied
with our country's terror.
My heart aches for trying to hold such pain
for so many days. I could not settle long in prayer,
dear God, but I was with you in brief spurts.
When I waited for the bus, I connected to all
as I gazed at the autumn sky
and breathed you into myself.
Intense gatherings with our Peace House community
considering our future are difficult but hopeful.
The poor are so caring about our place
and they care about the coordinators.
You, Holy Presence,
were in the midst of our sessions
bringing forth the energy and wisdom
of the group to unite us.
This Saturday morning
I am thoughtful and more settled.

It seems that this will be a blessed hermit day for me.
I step down the street to the Second Moon Cafe
and buy a small latte.
I take it outside and sit on the wooden bench
unoccupied by anyone but me.
I savor my coffee, the peaceful blue sky
and changing leaves across the street.
At this moment, I make friends
with everyone in my heart,
you most of all, Holy Presence.
You are so close and I thank you.

# 10. You Are the Calm in Our Midst

Yesterday was filled with violent
words and actions at Peace House.
God, I believe you were in our midst,
but such anger was difficult to bear.
All over the world the "sacred poem"
intended for us humans is rent apart
by violence that you, O God, never intended.

So many of your children live in fear,
dissipation, cruelty, and pain.
Gandhi wrote: "An eye for an eye ends up
making the whole world blind."
How can I, weak as I am, birth hope and nourishment
for myself and all of humankind?
Today, with your help, I vow in my heart
to bring some small gifts of loveliness
to this broken world.
Please kindle within me
your gracious fire, that I might extend its sparks
to the places in this world where the fierce agents
of war and violence dominate and snuff out
the inner fires you have instilled into all hearts.
May I model nonviolence in heart and mouth
wherever I go today.
May you, God of Calm, "show me your ways
and teach me your paths" of mercy and justice.

# 11. You Are My Blessed One

Holy One of Leisure Blessings,
I have an open space this mid-week
that I like to think of as "no-hurry" time.
Help me to move freely and consciously this day
doing what needs to be done
but with minimum urgency.
In Ed Hays' "Prayers for a Planetary Pilgrim,"
the Wednesday morning prayer asks
that we "reflect God's splendor"
as we move through the time given to us.
I must remember this phrase with thanksgiving.
What an honor to be born for this purpose!
It is a reflection that boosts me from
my early morning doldrums this day.
It is dark and cold outside,
and I had some hours of nervous sleep last night.
When I facilitate meditation at Peace House,
I ask at the beginning that all of us focus
on the Sacred within and around us.

"We are in holy time and holy space," I say,
"let us try to live this in our words and actions."
Direct me, Holy One of Leisure Blessings,
to maintain quiet within
and moments of awareness of my call
to "reflect your splendor" this day.

## 12. You Are the
## God of Laughter

My God of Fun and Laughter,
what enjoyment you injected into our lives last night
at our gathering of friends.
After such a stormy two weeks,
I felt the "dew from heaven drop down,"
and it isn't even close to Advent!
What a spirited sweep over all of us!
So many gatherings are laden with heavy agenda,
fitting into such small slots of time.
Help me, O Holy One of Laughter,
to extend this upbeat attitude
and lightheartedness throughout this day.
It will help me to lift myself and others
into a joyful aura and to work it into
the possible irksome happenings of today.

If things do become overwhelming,
remind me that I simply cannot allow myself
to fall into heavy gloom and then become crabby
with the Peace House Community and others.
Fun, foolishness, and frolic are sacraments for me,
though they are not listed in the catechism.
Thank you, God of Laughter, for such blessings.

# 13. You Are
## the God of Blessings

When I came home to my apartment yesterday,
God of Blessings, I went right to the window
hoping to feast on the brilliant orange, purple,
gold, and red coxcomb down in the courtyard.
I was so startled to see that it had been
cut down for the winter.
I just moved away from the window
not wanting to face the barren scene.
I sat in my chair and grieved
because this beauty had been taken from me,
this brightness for my tired heart.
I reflect on how you, God,
allow certain beauties to fade from our lives:
a dear one, security, good health,
only to soothe us with other gifts.
Gratitude for all I have received
is my prayer this morning.

My list begins with day one of my life.
I believe that we come forth into this world
to bless and to be blessed all the days of our lives.
My mother's birth waters were the first waters
to bless and sustain me.
Today "I count the ways" that you bless me.
Help me, Holy One, to realize gift after gift,
mutual blessings from moment to moment.
Sustain me when I can't find the blessings.
May I not miss the serendipities,
the surprises, as this day moves along.
I want to be one with you and all that is.
Great God of Blessings.

# 14. You Are a God Who Raises Up

God Who Raises Up,
I can sense this early Monday morning
that a darkness of heart has crept
into me during the night.
I was very despondent last evening over the
world scene of fear, violence, and terror.
Nations are returning evil with evil,
violence with violence.
Depression and anger over the victimization
of the vulnerable weighed upon me
and kept me awake for a long time.
I cried out to you and begged for deliverance.
In turmoil I left my bed and danced around my space,
hoping to throw off my dark feelings.
I pushed at the air, symbolically
moving them out the window.
God Who Raises Up, I do not want to be
a bent-over, bitter woman
operating on negative energy all day.

Please raise my awareness of
your presence in and around me.
Help me to be nonviolent in thought and behavior.
Illuminate, please, my psyche of darkness
and help me to be open to the loveliness of this day.
May I pause at least five times today
and give you thanks for the pleasures in my life
including yourself most of all.

# 15. You Are God of All That Is

Dear God, Lifegiver, this morning I awoke at 1:45.
My mother gave birth to me at two o'clock
in the morning 79 years ago today.
What were your thoughts about my coming,
my dear mother? You were always frail.
Did you think that one more child at that time
in your life would be too much for you?
Or did you rejoice because this girl
was welcome after four boys?
Perhaps you worried that I would not
come forth alive because your first baby died enroute.
Thank you, God, Birther of All That Is.
Today I am so grateful to be on this Mother Earth.
I ponder the richness of my many years.
Light and darkness have followed me around,
taking turns to give me their blessings.
"Let me count the ways," wrote Elizabeth Browning.
I began this morning to count;
I scarce could take those blessings in.

From my first bicycle to yesterday's last bus ride,
the gifts outnumber the stars of the largest galaxy.
O Great Giver of All That Is
plus the Yet to Come, I dance and sing
loud enough to wake all my neighbors.

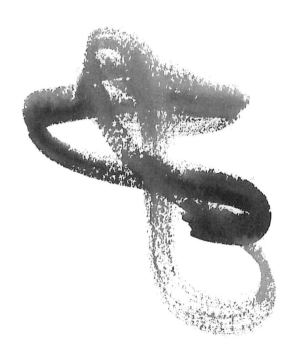

 # 16. You Are the God of Calm

Great God of Calm, although this blue sky
autumn day looks promising weather-wise,
I feel unsteady in my body/soul.
There are people who appear to be
sowing seeds of discontent and divisiveness,
and I am frightened. Help me so I won't let
suspicions distract me or eat me up.
"Where there is hatred, let me sow love."
Dorothy Day wrote, "The final work is love."
I must realize that even though I try
to confront the issues head-on,
I cannot control the people who seem to want friction.
But I do not know their hearts, really.
Perhaps they are not even aware of the pain
they arouse in others who mean well.
Give me a tender heart, Great God of Calm.
"Make me a channel of your peace."

Direct some energy of your totally
nonviolent heart to me this day.
I do not want to feel the same kind of spite
I am sensing in others.
Walk closely with me, God,
and warm my deepest heart.
Move me to embrace with caution and kindness
the people I'm upset with.
O God of Calm,
hold me in your embrace
that I too might be calm.

# 17. You Are God Among Us

God Among Us, this morning small, white flakes
sweep across my window at a swift pace.
A snowstorm is predicted.
The scene makes me shiver. I ponder:
are weather changes under your control, God?
I have surmised that controlling floods,
hurricanes, tornadoes are not in your job description.
Yet they are referred to in the law books
and in the media as "acts of God."

What an affront to say that you would
destroy anything with force.
Nor do I believe that you are to blame for what
we humans do to one another and ourselves.
Acts of terror, violence, injustice, oppression
are not of your making.
Was it Robert Browning who said,
"God's in his heaven;
all's right with the world"?
All is right? Where?
God, you are amid all that is,
not on some throne above the world you created.
What appears obvious to me is that
you are within and among us at all times
to comfort, support, love,
embrace, forgive, prod,
energize, enlighten, and turn us
toward your Sacred Self.
And of course to spur us into dance.

# 18. You Are the God of Wonders

Dear God of Ice and Cold,
winter came in the night,
howling its way, bringing ten inches of snow
from the Rockies into our city.
From my window I can see
the top half of an evergreen
against the building across from mine.
God of Wonder and Artistry,
I delight in this winter gift,
which is truly awesome and wonder-filled.
All is transformed.
Yesterday these same branches stood unadorned,
though lovely in their bareness.
In earlier years of my life
I would have thought that a focus on anything
but purely you would have been a distraction
to be confessed in the confessional.

Today I can truly cry out:
God, it is you I see in that
wondrous snow-touched tree.
Thank you, God of Wonders,
for calling me from the gloom of the confessional
to Your cosmic revelation
of a single upper half of a winter tree.

# 19. You Are My Strength

It is early morning, Great God of Strength.
My left ear will be the death of me
and my lower jaw is throbbing with pain.
Accompany me this day, O Holy One,
lest I think I am far above the conditions
that ordinary folks suffer,
lest I dash my foot against a stone of pride
and delusion about my limitations.
Great God of Strength,
this week I have buckled under
from too much conflict in myself and others.
I must move away from this heavy stress
and the constant needs of others.
But I don't want to retire.
I especially don't want
to move into our retirement home.
I am still too healthy to slip away
from the real world and fall into
the path of comfort and isolation.

I don't want to turn my back
on the miseries I encounter every day.
I fear that any seclusion that will veil from me
the street world, the homelessness,
and the harsh realities that so many
of our brothers and sisters in the world experience
will dim my memory of them
and my prayer for them will cease.
I never want that to happen.
Strengthen me, keep me going this day,
Great God of Strength.

# 20. You Are
# the God of Mercy

Today my back and legs ache,
not as before when I could not tolerate it,
but enough to make me feel uncomfortable.
Lately, Great God of Mercy,
I have been so aware of the
corporate pain in the world:
the dreadful disaster of war,
the thousands of adults who were abused as children,
the paralyzed people,
people who are in mental anguish,
children who are starving.
Now I have a reminder that I am part
of this pained humankind.
I ask you, God of Mercy and Compassion,
to help me find more bondedness
with all of your people in pain.
I want to grow in compassion
and understanding of all those in my life.

Also, help me to realize more fully
that I am in you and you in me.
Teach me how I can become
more reflective of your gracious self
through the sufferings that come into my life.
I know you don't will pain,
so help me to find ways to relieve
what I feel in my back and legs today.
Please have mercy and compassion
on all your children all over the world this day.
You are indeed the God of Mercy.

# 21. You Are
## the God of Flowers

A bouquet of irises from our garden
graces the living room.
I have been in a slump,
but as I contemplate one single flower
in all its glory, I am lifted into you,
God, Creator of the Flowers,
  where I revel in awe of your gracious gifts.
In love you designed this flower
  with delicate shades of violet and purple.
The iris whispers from her deepest soul,
"Look upon me and just be.
This is a holy moment of grace for you.
I am here to touch your heart with my dignity
and gracefulness and to call you
to reflect on your own dignity and grace.
We are sisters, you and I."
Thank you, God of Flowers, for my sister iris.

# 22. You Are My Support

I am never powerless,
for you are my Rock and my Support.
Even though the circumstances I'm connected to
are not mine to resolve directly,
I can still do something.
I have the power to move my energies
into tune with you, Holy One,
to unite my heart with your heart.
It is possible for me to pray earnestly
for those in my life who are suffering sickness,
struggling in their relationships, their poverty,
dealing with disappointments and anxieties.
Even when I seem to be imprisoned
within the walls of my apparent ineffectiveness,
my feelings of vulnerability and hurt,
I can move with you, O God,
who created me in your likeness, and I can be powerful.
Hold me now, loving Rock of Support,
and keep me in your truth.

# 23. You Are a Faithful God

Today, dear Faithful God,
I feel that I am emerging from a struggle
that pinned me in pain for several days.
I am wiser since I've gone through it
and surely also more graced.
Those days of confinement helped me
to know my power
even as I was just treading water
minute by minute, day by day.
I even feel a little heady about doing so well,
considering the circumstances.
You never left me during any of that time,
and I thank you, my Faithful God.
Help me to hold on to the lessons
my pain has taught me,
and the gifts my pain has given me:
patience, compassion toward others,
and trust in your faithfulness.

# 24. You Are My Bright Light

The sun is moving into my space
here in the living room, filling me
and everything in the room
with its warmth and brightness.
It casts shadows, too, and then
withdraws behind clouds in the east.
I can see them between the branches
of the evergreen tree outside my window.
Now the sun returns, and I feel that you,
my God of Bright Light, are saying,
"Allow my radiance to hold you
as the shadows of your day come and go.
I will be with you when the bleak moments
of this day darken your spirit.
Return to your brightened space of this morning
and know that my love never leaves you."
I call from my shadowy depths to you,
Warming God, God of Light,
and let myself bask in your radiance.

# 25. You Are God of Mindfulness

Today, God of Mindfulness,
I want to practice contemplation
in the drinking of a glass of water,
the taking of a breath,
the use of my good legs as I walk,
my eyes as I take the bus to work.
Let me take nothing for granted
and help me to be in awe of the ordinary.
As I look upon people today,
help me to feel kind to them and close to them
in our common human struggle.
Lead me to look with benevolence
upon those I pass on the street,
that my loving energy toward them
might help charge the universe.
Let me savor the uniqueness of each moment
as a precious time of grace.
May I be mindful of you today
in all the ways you dwell in others.

# 26. You Are My Refuge

Yesterday my heart was storm-tossed.
High waves of agony threw me violently,
and I cried out to you for relief.
Today, Loving God, my rescuer, my refuge,
you have mercifully heard me,
gathered me to sweet moments of tranquility.
I savor this time and revel in its sensuous peace.
The agony has left me weak physically,
but strength of spirit satisfies and excites me.
I have a taste of merciful and lovely calm,
a gift I want to hold forever.
I am swelling with the exuberance of being alive.
A bud on our African violet has opened
since I began to write, and I hold it as a sign
that I too am opening to a gracious sampling
of your great love and calm.
Today I call out my thanksgiving to you,
O Merciful God of Calm and Compassion.
You are my joy; you are my refuge.

# 27. You Are the God of Peace

As I go forth into this day, Holy God,
I make a commitment to reflect in simple ways
on your heart of Love and Peace.
I want to walk with your broken ones
as a peer in life's pain
and as their sister in peace and joy.
Teach me to be more loving, more patient,
more tolerant, and more accepting of those
who are close to me in my life
at home and at work.
I ask for a heart on fire with zeal
for justice and peacemaking,
though sometimes I'm now
limited to less active ways of doing this.
Strengthen me so I won't lose heart,
especially when war, famine,
homelessness, and greed are so apparent.
Call me to nonviolence daily
that I might be a "channel of your peace."

# 28. You Are God of Suffering Ones

Today I feel angry and hurt,
my Loving Comforter God.
I don't know where to go with my feelings.
I cry out to you to hold me and give me comfort.
I try to turn over to you my pain.
As I work at this, I unite my humanness
with that of all suffering people
and I feel bonded with them.
The reality of universal pain
overwhelms me at this moment,
but I see myself in this great pool
of common anguish trying to hear
what you are asking of me.
Help me to release the anger
that keeps me from knowing your love
and hearing your voice.
Bless all who suffer this day,
dear God of Suffering Ones.

# 29. You Are My Weaver God

My thoughts are unfocused today,
Loving Weaver God.
They leap around in unconnected
flashes and pieces.
I feel scattered and unsettled.
Gather me into your embrace
and let me know that I am
an integral part of the universe
in which you take great delight.
Weave me together this day
that I might recognize the warp and woof
of my life as an integrated design
reflecting the gracious love
in which you hold me.
Walk with me today,
leap with me today,
dance with me today,
loving Weaver of my life.

# 30. You Are
# a God of Compassion

Help me, Holy Compassionate God,
to embrace the shadow side
of those with whom I live and work.
When I am irritated by someone's behavior,
lead me to pray for that person with compassion.
Don't let me afflict myself
by dwelling on these irritations
because this will sap my strength.
If I need to confront someone,
strengthen me to do so graciously,
not with sharpness or harshness.
I know I need to unite
my own shadow self with all
who struggle on this earth
to find their way to peace with you.
If my tongue slips and I utter hurtful words,
temper me with patience and acceptance
of my companions on this path to you.

And when I hurt others
because of my human weakness,
help me to ask for forgiveness
with a humble and contrite heart.
Holy God of Compassion,
may I love others this day
"with passion," and peace.

# 31. You Are
# My Gracious Creator

Buds on my African violet
are once again close to opening.
I am in awe of this mystery, Gracious Creator,
and I pause to give thanks
that I have eyes to witness this unfolding.
I am grateful too that I have eyes
to see the faces of the beloved ones
who walk with me through my life.
And eyes to read the scriptural words
of all the writers who draw me closer
to the reality of life's beauty and pain.
My eyes window for me the green on the trees,
the children riding past on their bicycles.
I ask you, Gracious Creator of all I see,
to bless my eyes that I might not miss
what will enrich me this day.
Then beckon me to give thanks
that you have so wondrously fashioned my eyes.

## 32. You Are a Source of All

Gracious and Loving Source of All,
I strive to be in tune with you this day.
Hold me close and speak hopeful
and comforting words to me.
Dissolve my fears and place within me
a peaceful trust in you and in
your continued presence and care.
Share with me your gifts of
gentle love, compassion, and peace.
Help me to embrace nonviolence this day,
and if I am called upon to confront
unjust systems in church or society today,
give me the courage to do so.
Help me to be wholehearted
in pursuing your desires for me.
You are my Source,
my Gracious and Loving Source.

 ## 33. You Are God of Radiance

It seems as though I am waiting
for something to happen
that will give me heart,
like an exciting letter or phone call.
Although I know that the radiant sun
and May greenery outside my window
are sufficient to thrill me to the bone,
I am hankering for more.
I ask you, Loving Radiance,
help me to revel in the loveliness
of this spring day and not to look
for further excitement.
Pour into me the gift of deep satisfaction
with this moment's gifts, which are surely
sufficient to carry me through this day—
with courage and perhaps even enthusiasm.
Help me, God of Loving Radiance,
to give witness to your presence within me this day.

# 34. You Are My Rock

Loving God of Strength, my Rock,
today I ask for the vision
to see the direction you want me to go.
I feel handicapped
by my anxiety and lack of calm.
I want to focus quietly on your presence
in my life at this very moment.
Help me to sink trustfully into your arms
and let go of my gnawing
concerns and unrest.
Your gracious and loving heart
is here for me if only I would
just let go and become attuned to you completely.
Only you can relieve me.
Help my heart to beat with yours in all that I do.
You are my loving and sustaining God of Strength.
You give me strength and courage
when I need it most.
What would I do without you!

# 35. You Are the God of Joy

Dear God of Joy, a feeling of heaviness
overwhelms me this day.
I am weighed down by negative thoughts
that upset me and snuff out the peace
you gave me yesterday.
What can I do to regain it?
I ask you to help me focus
on your gracious gifts to me,
especially your gifts of compassion,
joy, patience, and courage.
I savor each one and thank you
for blessing me so uniquely.
Now that I have recalled what
strengthens me in my life,
I ask you to help me focus intently
on your generosity and to draw energy
from your gifts that I might be
lifted out of my doldrums.

O God, Intimate Friend and Giver of Joy,
stay beside me this day.
Call me out of this heaviness of heart
and let me bask in your
lightsome energy and deep joy.

# 36. You Are a God of Justice

I am depressed about the violence in the world,
my Holy and Blessed God of Justice.
Right now I am not physically able to go
to protests and demonstrations
at the sites of the perpetrators of war and violence.

I'm too old and too tired.
Yet, I ask your help in creating
a nonviolent heart within me.
Let me become more attuned
to your heart of goodness and peace.
Help me to replace resentful and spiteful thoughts
with forgiveness and gracious acceptance.
Guide me in ways of understanding
that the misery that prompts
violence against me comes from the struggles
people are experiencing in their own lives.
Keep me from retaliation
in words that will deepen their pain
and only provoke more violence.
Create in me a heart that will
reflect your graciousness,
dear Blessed One, God of Justice,
and let peace be born once again within me.

# 37. You Are a God of Healing

This day I hold out to you
the people in my circle of home, work,
and friendship who are in pain.
Holy Healer, hold each of them close
and assure them of their worth.
Lift from their despair
those who have given up hope.
Ease the discomfort of those who feel sick and weary.
Comfort the disturbed, the depressed, the anxious.
As I hold out each name
I ask you to send them
the energy and courage they need
to endure their physical pain
and all their life struggles.
I feel sister to all these sick and suffering
members of my earth family
and ask gracious relief and hope for them.
And for myself as well.

# 38. You Are God of Mystery

For such a long time, Great God of Mystery,
I lived by the official catechism,
assuming that it was the only way to go.
Although I can still quote
most of the questions and answers,
I don't refer to them on a daily basis.
Nor do I deny them outright
or cast away all that I have been taught.
I fully recognize that some of those who
passed these teachings along to me
lived in deep faith and mirrored
your compassion and justice.
The holy lives of so many who have gone before me
are the enlightenment that I now carry with me daily.
They are the living doctrines,
the living catechism,
and their example fills me
with your holy presence.
Thank you, Great God of Mystery,
for revealing this Blessed truth to me.

# 39. You Are
# My Attentive One

I ask you, Attentive One,
to give me a sense of your presence during my day.
Help me to absorb reverently
the moments you give me
and find in them a wealth of meaning.
Keep me from moving too fast.
Hold me gently in the NOW
that I might not miss its gifts and graces.
If any moments of my day seem tedious,
enliven my heart to see their richness as well.
Unfold for me the significance
of a routine task as being an opportunity
to know you and your gracious creation more fully.
I realize that if I try to see, hear, and touch attentively,
I will live more fully.
I want to become alive to the time
you give me because it is so sacred.
May I be attentive to you, Holy Attentive One,
in every moment of this day.

# 40. Still God of the Dance

Dance, dance,
wherever you may be;
The God of the Dance
will set your soul free.
And if by chance
your body is too lame,
dance in your heart
brightened by the flame
of God's energizing love
freely bestowed with unheard of
grace and goodness and ease
Come dance, come dance, please.
The God of the Dance will
take away your every fear
and lead you from darkness
into a light that is ever near.
Dance, dance,
wherever you may be;
The God of the Dance
will set your soul free.

# Autobiography

In 1923 I came into this world to bless and be blessed. Minneota, Minnesota was the small southwestern town that received me a few years before the Great Depression. I was a public school kid. I grew up with four brothers, three older, one younger. My parents were Katherine Welch and William P. Tillemans. We five kids literally grew up in the shadow of our church, which was one block from our house. St. Edward's Catholic Church was pastored by Father Philip Casey, our patriarch, who made clear to us that he was in charge of his flock. We did not question him but revered him nevertheless. His heavy Irish brogue and stately appearance were distinctive, and he was pastoral in his own way.

My parents paid for nine years of piano lessons. Although I loved to play, I did not keep up my practicing through the years. Though I can't read a note of Mozart, Chopin, Rachmaninoff, or Debussy, the music I learned remains in my head and heart. When I hear my old pieces on public radio, I am bonded with the richly gifted composers and our old piano in its special room in our dear old house on Jefferson Street in Minneota. My life was centered in family, church, catechism classes, piano, Girl Scouts, and friends with whom I invented school plays, circuses, and carnivals during my growing up years.

I guess one could say that I was quite a pious girl and teenager. For confirmation my godmother gave me a copy of *The Catholic Girl's Guide*. I took the text quite seriously and even went into a period of scrupulosity as I pondered the examination of conscience. My mother, noting my misery, took me aside and said, "Your religion must be a pleasure to you." It took me a long time to really believe this, but I did recover from the pain of scrupulosity shortly after my mother's comforting words. After high school I went to the College of St. Catherine in St. Paul, Minnesota, majoring in Library Science and minoring in English and Sociology. I avoided education courses because I had a terrible fear of being a teacher. My college transcript was less than stellar, but I did get As in creative writing and religion. My colleagues would ask me to help them prepare for exams and to guide them in theme writing. And to think most of them were graduates of Catholic high schools!

I had never been exposed to economics, world conditions, or politics. However, the moderator of Our Lady's Sodality directed us young women to go out by twos and find "the poor" on Saturday afternoons. My roommate and I took a county Road B bus and visited the Ramsey County Poor Farm. It was my introduction to poor people in every bent and gnarled shape, emotionally distraught, without anything to their names. I held these people in my heart with deep concern. Little did I know what turn my life would take twenty-eight years later.

After graduation I worked as a librarian in a neuropsychiatric hospital. I wheeled a bookcart to many locked wards where I might find one or two patients who wanted to read. My social life was eventful, but I became bored and found little to excite me. It was at this time that I experienced an inner beckoning to become a Sister of St. Joseph of Cardondelet, the order that had taught me piano lessons for so many years and later educated me in college. I was very secretive about the whole process and also embarrassed to have anyone know what I was up to. Was it some sort of immature piety, I wonder, as I reflect upon my behavior of so many years ago?

Although life in the convent was very strict, I stuck it out, clowning my way through with a lot of anxiety. But I have gracious

68

memories of those years too. Since we were largely a teaching and nursing order, and I wanted to be neither, I wondered what they would do with me. Well, they sent me right back to college to pick up educational credits at St. Catherine's. After that it was teaching and library work from 1950 to 1974. Since I have a very dominant anxiety gene, there were many hospitalizations and time-out periods. I call them "crack-ups" and try to add some humor and acceptance to those rough years.

When I was recovering from my worst struggle, I saw an ad in our community newsletter for someone to work at the Free Store. I asked the permission of a most trusting provincial in my order. Without hesitation she gave me the nod, literally, as she was just leaving her building when I was coming through the door. I blurted out my request as we met enroute. Indeed it was a nod, because it seemed to her that no words were necessary. My anxiety gene remained active amid the chaos of sorting clothes, running to the phone, and meeting the needs of the very poor who came to shop free. But I had no more total breakdowns or hospitalizations even when I became overwhelmed by the demands of the work. After ten and a half years at the Free Store, I knew that I must leave. That decision prompted me to pursue my dream of several years: to create a community day center for poor and homeless people who wanted a place to be with others seeking spirituality, friendship, and affirmation.

In my dreams I called this place Peace House. I solicited old friends and family to help me finance this new venture. With the approval of my CSJ leaders and the support of folks who could help me plan what would happen in this Peace House, I began to look for a storefront in the poor areas of Minneapolis. By chance someone alerted me to a possible site. It was an old building in the center of a neighborhood in which were housed several agencies for the poor. I did not have in mind any formal structure for Peace House. I wanted it to be simple, safe, and friendly, a gathering center for sharing stories, praying together for those who were falling through the cracks.

Neighbors and our alderman objected strongly to what they considered another social agency. At a neighborhood meeting the pressure against me was so strong that I really gave up, called the owner in Florida to ask him to release me from the lease. His answer, was "Don't give up so easily. Look at all Jesus suffered." My silent response was "Yeah, and look what happened to him!" The Dairy Queen owner next to the house had stood up at the meeting and said, "I don't want Ms. Tillemans' customers clobbering mine," followed by, "nor do I want the pure image of Dairy Queen tainted."

Well, with the encouragement of the pastor at St. Stephen's Church nearby, I mustered the courage to move in. When the guests had all left after a prayer service to mark the opening of Peace House, I sat down in the one upholstered chair. I waited from noon until 4:00 PM, and not a single person dropped in. After about two weeks and the purchase of a coffee pot and doughnuts, people started to come in twos and threes.

Since the beginning, we have had meditation at 11:30 AM, many times on what the lives of the homeless people are like, how they survive amid police brutality and lack of shelter space. We emphasize participation in the housekeeping of the day, affirm one another, work on nonviolence, and pray for our needs. All of us volunteer coordinators have been inspired by the wisdom of the women and men who gather daily at Peace House.

Mutual mentoring has been a part of our ministry since the beginning, which is my idea for the beginning of structural change in society. Many of our people are assisted in getting into treatment. We direct people to resources where help for housing and jobs is offered. Our Peace House has become a learning center for grade and high school students, as well as those in college. For me it has often been strenuous work, but ever so enriching and loving.

In the 80s and early 90s I realized more and more the plight of the poor and the oppression laid upon them by our culture. I joined demonstrations at Honeywell and at downtown official office buildings. I went down to the School of the Americas to protest the training of soldiers, from both the United States and Central America, who were responsible for the murders of so many civilians as well as church women and men. My sister-housemate and I decided to give space to refugees from Guatemala and El Salvador. These were very rich years for me, and I hold them dear.

Since the Second Vatican Council, I have done a lot of writing, much in satiric verse. I have self-published several small books, conveying with humor and a bit of bite the pomp of the Catholic hierarchical system. My last one I called *Questions of a Cradle Catholic* in which I puzzled over nearly everything I had ever been taught. How can the males of the church know what we are to believe and not believe? It is my conviction that everyone has some of the truth. The official catechism is the interpretation of some scholars and theologians—they too have only a part of the truth.

So I dance every day to the truths that express for me what makes sense: giving love, caring for others in their needs, working for justice, sharing tenderness, accepting the things I cannot change, working with the poor who must often face insurmountable obstacles, caring for Earth and all its children.

# Of Related Interest

## Three Books by Melannie Svoboda:

### Abundant Treasures
*Meditations on the Many Gifts of the Spirit*
The 51 gifts in this book include quotations, meditations, prayers, and reflection questions to help readers focus on and appreciate the abundant riches present in their lives.
0-89622-999-8, 132 pp, $9.95 (J-46)

### Rummaging for God
*Seeking the Holy in Every Nook and Cranny*
Contains 100 rummagings, that is, short meditations that grew out of the author's own experience. Questions and short closing prayers and source and topic indexes help facilitate the reader's own rummaging.
0-89622-943-2, 136 pp, $9.95 (J-21)

### Everyday Epiphanies
*Seeing the Sacred in Every Thing*
Offers 175 short stories with topics ranging from setting the table, getting the mail, rain, and working, to the uncommon occasions that we all look forward to and relish.
0-89622-730-8, 192 pp, $12.95 (B-45)

*Plucking the Strings…*
### A Personal Psalm Journal
Joan Metzner

Everyday events and a full range of emotions provide the grist for these beautifully formed psalms. Perfect for use on retreat, for morning or evening prayer, or for any of those special times set aside for prayer.
0-89622-733-2, 120 pp, $9.95 (B-74)

**TWENTY-THIRD PUBLICATIONS**
185 WILLOW STREET • PO BOX 180 • MYSTIC, CT 06355
TEL: 1-800-321-0411 • FAX: 1-800-572-0788
Bayard  E-MAIL: ttpubs@aol.com • www.twentythirdpublications.com